# *Are you chasing someone else's dream?*

Covey Filmore

# Contents

# Chapter 1: How it all began

The title is straightforward, but the answer is not, for several reasons. As we proceed, we will delve into several of these factors. Many various events shape us as children as we grow through our childhoods, adolescence, young adulthood, and beyond. We learn as youngsters through our senses what we see, taste, hear, feel, and smell. These instincts, along with our parents, grandparents, aunts and uncles, who may or may not be in your group during these formative years, comprise our basic operating system. When you first tasted something, you didn't like, you knew you didn't want to eat it again. Even when you tried it in numerous settings, it just didn't work for you. This also applies to your other senses and other things you've grown to love or loathe over the years and seasons of your life. As youngsters, we often have what is thought to be a personality, which is sometimes admired and managed with care. Depending on the family dynamic, the present may be overlooked and perceived as disrespectful or unappreciative. This will be the primary emphasis of this chapter. A child that is nurtured for their innate talents can go a long way with just encouragement and that talent. If a child loves to sing, play games, or be outside from an early age, these are all clues that this child is drawn to these activities, and with correct supervision, this might be this child's purpose, or at least a piece of that purpose.

The youngster who enjoys singing but is constantly advised to be quiet will soon stop singing; the child who enjoys playing games will eventually lose interest when there is no one to play with; and the child who enjoys being outside will eventually refuse to go outside when everyone else does. It takes effort to see what that child would see. Many times, as parents, we are so overwhelmed just trying to make it that our children fall through the cracks, and we wonder why they are suddenly having behavioral issues, or why they are shutting down, and your relationship with them seems to be becoming more and more like the relationship you had with your parents, which is the very last thing you ever wanted, or maybe you had a wonderful childhood and you are trying to recreate it for your child. If we delve deeper, we may find that the same thing happened to you. You were so excited to share a thought or something you had created as a child, and you just knew that once the person you showed it to saw this masterpiece, they would finally understand not only you, but many of the things you had been misunderstood about, but instead you didn't even get all the way through the process before you were shot down or before you realized they weren't even listening. You recall the moment vividly, and believe it or not, that is when something inside of you broke.

You had no idea what to do next as a child. You may have shown your pals at school and they shared your joy, but home was where you really wanted it to be this fantastic thing and it wasn't. This is the point at which you adjusted certain things in yourself to be okay. You're not even conscious that you're doing it as a child. Some children shut down and just focus on other things, leaving that concept in the back of their minds. It comes up over time, you work on it, but it doesn't really go anywhere, so you put it back on your mental shelf and go about your business.

Others act out and become very different children, and ultimately completely different persons. They are never the same after that letdown, and they spend the rest of their lives trying to find out where and when everything went wrong. On the opposite end of the spectrum, you have a child whose parents were enthusiastic about listening to them sing or play games with them, and where outside time was a daily or weekend event. This child succeeded in school and did well with assistance from not only the family dynamic but also a large community of support. This child was expressive and confident, and he or she went on to pursue his or her aspirations and become a well-rounded individual. It only needed a little more effort here and there to ensure that the child understood the significance of his or her dreams and that they could be realized. Not only could those ambitions be realized, but assistance would be provided along the process, offering a sense of ease and comfort during the stressful teen years, difficult young adult years, and eventually prosperous, confident adult years and beyond.

Before I go any further, let me state unequivocally that it is not anyone's blame that this conclusion is frequently not attained simply because there is no reference book. Many times, we do the best we can as parents, and our parents did the best they could, and we can go down the line to our great great grandparents, who did the best they could with the programming and what they had. Each generation basically carried the very best attributes from the preceding ones all the way down to you, and now you have a once-in-a-lifetime opportunity to shift the flow of your family's triumphs, at least the ones in your household. You only get one life, and it is everyone's goal to make it the greatest one possible while not destroying our children or anyone else. Being a good person is a great place to start. Many times, as humans, we simply misunderstand one another, and that one misunderstanding will cause you to dislike a certain person, and you may even recruit others to dislike that person because you don't like them or don't understand them because of that misunderstanding during your initial meeting. This could also be related to your childhood and how you digest unfamiliar information.

It's interesting because it's usual to detest or loathe something we don't understand instead of spending the effort to figure out why. It's simply too much effort to ask a few questions in order to acquire clarification in a scenario. Have you ever spent time with someone you thought was quirky or peculiar at first, only to discover that they were a very pleasant person with whom you shared certain interests? Or have you ever worked with someone and everyone said negative things about them so you felt that way solely because of word of mouth, then you had to do an assignment together and you found them to be so interesting in such a short period of time that you didn't understand why everyone said the things they said? People would empathize with the things they were told by others if they took the time to genuinely get to know others. They were induced to feel this way as a result of someone else's misinterpretation of that individual. It's as simple as that. But, unfortunately, for many of us, simple is simply too complicated and tough to do.

Simplicity is overcomplicated early in our lives by the same variables that we covered, and we spend a lot of time as we get older just trying to make things a bit simpler for ourselves, not recognizing that we are the ones who piled the to-do list so high in the first place. Life is intended to be a journey to uncover the truest version of ourselves and then grow into that person, and once you know you've done that, you expand and share your gift, purpose, etc. with the rest of the world. If you're reading this as an adult, you know that you can't go back in time and change who you are today. Can't you? You can truly heal your inner child by returning to the point where the trauma or derailing of your adolescence began in your adult life. If you're wondering where to begin, the solution is simpler than you think and will be covered in the following chapter.

# Chapter 2: Work with Your Inner-Child

To begin, I understand that many people have never heard of an inner-child or how to work on or with one, so this should be interesting to say the least. Your inner-child is constantly present. Maybe you get a little too excited when you hear your favorite song, or maybe you smell a fragrance that reminds you of a time when you were very young, and you remember every detail of the moment when you first smelled that wonderful aroma, and every time you smell it, it transports you right back to that time frame. You have feelings that are linked to sad memories, just like you had in Chapter One, when you were delighted to share groundbreaking news with your family only to be disregarded and disappointed by their replies. That could be a key moment that needs to be acknowledged and worked through before you can move forward. For what it's worth, they were useful at the time we put them in place because we used them to protect ourselves from whatever was trying to hurt us at the time, but the issue was never addressed, and we just allowed more and more hurtful moments to pile on top of those things, and nothing was ever addressed. And when we tried to talk things through, we were often met with more pain or negative reactions, so we just buried it all deep inside and it came up here and there, but it was truly only your problem because you never had anyone to help you work it all the way through so that it was no longer a sore spot.

The first step in inner-child work is determining where and why it all began. Finding the answer isn't difficult because we often have a recollection that cycles through our minds pretty frequently, not every day, but frequently enough that you are conscious of its anguish. Maybe something a parent or sibling said in passing that remained with you and you've replayed it in your head trying to figure out what they truly meant. You may have inquired what they meant throughout the years and received an answer that seemed hollow or withheld the element that would provide you with the clarity you wanted. Or perhaps a teacher or a classmate at school did or said something that altered you and has been with you all this time, and you're not sure why it made you feel the way it did, but here you are, attempting to move past it in order to finally have peace of mind. Many times, we believe that it must be a catastrophic occurrence, such as abuse or a major struggle, even if these may occur. That is not correct. A single sentence can throw you off course and you won't even realize it. The easiest way to describe it is like a tear in the fabric of who you are that gradually becomes a rip since the hole was initially so small that it didn't appear to require any repair. The good news is that the rip can be fixed, and you won't even notice that there was ever a rip or any other form of defect on the fabric of who you're becoming.

Once you've identified the time or moments in question, feel the feelings that come with them, even if they hurt, and address them before letting them go. We'll go into more detail about this process in coming chapters, but for now, pinpoint the source of your inner turmoil, what caused you to veer off path. Once you've identified the root, not only can you begin to heal, but you'll also be able to start reconstructing the truest version of yourself. It may seem strange to consider that something you enjoyed as a youngster may become a passion or a part of your life's mission, but if you truly think about it, where else would it come from? Some things, of course, are generational, such as families of doctors, attorneys, teachers, and so on. It works the same way in that case as well; the family guided and the child responded; if it was a natural calling for that child, the child followed it all the way through and it became their profession; on the other hand, you have families who pushed their children into family situations that had been passed down through generations, and it just wasn't a fit, and the person was miserable trying to live up to an expectation placed on them by their family. The interaction is complicated because you may admire all aspects of the family tradition but not desire it for yourself. It can be challenging to find your own middle ground and stick to it when you don't know whether or not your family will back you.

This is a direct example of chasing someone else's dream; your family truly wants to set you up for a wonderful future and life, but they don't realize that this isn't what you want for your life. The stress you put on yourself by not being able to openly express your wishes and worries to your family might last into adulthood. Most of the time, once you get the guts to express your worries, you cause a schism in the family since your family is frequently split and sees your refusal to follow the framework, they have planned for you as disrespect. Things can mend and heal over time, and you'll be glad you took the decisions you did. This one is a little more straightforward to deal with. However, for those who are only now becoming aware of the damage and want to take the necessary measures to heal and become whole, it all begins here. Your inner-child is very important and is a huge part of who you are; as adults, we usually have our inner-child under control and navigate through our daily lives; it may or may not pop out when exciting things happen during our days, such as a raise at work or a celebration for a loved one when you're in your element. Your inner-child is the part of you that is in charge of imagination and creativity, and most of the time we either go there for inspiration or we drive ourselves insane trying to achieve it through other methods that usually fall short.

Doing the work to heal this extremely vital part of yourself is critical, and it starts with realizing that something is lacking and wanting to do something about it. Once you reach this point, the cognitive process of going through your life begins. It may begin with tiny patches of your life as much as you can recall at a time, but you will be astonished at how much more comes through with each memory. The details you will remember will be so detailed that you will be able to recollect the entire moment as if you were watching a movie from a long time ago; some will be joyous and loving, while others will be painful and sad. All of this is required to come to the point of reassembling yourself and becoming more whole than you have ever been. When you find the right moment in your life, you will know it because the emotion it evokes in you will be so strong that you will be unable to deny it. Some of us remember that exact moment and can replay it like a hit song on the radio today. However, when it comes to you, sit in the feeling of it for a bit, feeling all of the emotions related with it, and you will know when you are ready to go forward because you will be tired of hanging on to the energy associated with it. There is no right or wrong way to do this; just do what seems right to you, and you will be able to face something that has been a huge part of you for a long time.

It would be ideal if this never happened, but there are far more injured people on the streets than there are complete. You are just ready to begin the process of living a better life and becoming the person you were always intended to be, and this is what we were all meant to do. For those who received direction from childhood on, they are the friends who are always so upbeat, whose families are so supportive, who earned good grades in school and then secured a decent job later in life, and for whom everything just seemed to fall into place. They are always so supportive of you, but they don't know how to help you through this because it is something they have never experienced. And you've always admired them, maybe even envied them, because these are the things you wanted for yourself but didn't know where to start. To be honest, there was no way for you to know the steps when you wanted them because you didn't know what was wrong. Life has a way of showing us exactly what we need, just when we need it. If you're a parent reading this, you have two facets to consider: healing for yourself and getting back on track, and providing your child or children with what they need to be well-rounded and whole for their futures.

# Chapter 3: Letting Go

It appears to be simple; simply let go and everything will be fine. To be honest, if it were that easy, many of us would have done it by now and be enjoying our best lives. The weight of the hurt that many of us carry takes a while to unload, and only you can decide how long this process will take. It makes no difference how old or young you are, how you were raised, or how badly you want to complete the task. What matters is that you start the process and feel the weight lift off of you in the ways necessary to experience progress, and then you will feel revitalized and everything will just seem to change. If you need content to refer to, you can get it from focus groups, social media, gurus, books, films, and so on. There is no shortage of resources to assist you in becoming the best version of yourself. When you start bringing up the hurts, both good and bad, you will notice things in your daily life that feed the narrative you are attempting to escape. Sometimes we need a complete renovation to recharge our lives and begin again. Also, if you are having difficulty finding time for yourself, remember that nothing will change in your life until you make time for the change that you desire. There will always be debts to pay, assignments to complete, or new challenges to face. You must make time for yourself. Many times, we are so used to placing ourselves last for the sake of those we care about that we are unaware of the harm we are creating and that we are operating on empty.

Another way to look at it is that if you don't make time for yourself and your desires, who will? You will discover that you have always had the power to do and become whatever you have ever sought in your life the moment you commit to not only healing but also loving all of yourself. You can't keep running on empty for everyone else while putting nothing into yourself. After a while, you will exhaust yourself and cause more harm than good. Letting go doesn't have to take up a lot of your time to begin with if you can just sit and contemplate for 5 or 10 minutes, and it frequently helps to journal or meditate so that you can clear your mind with meditation and interpret your feelings in the present with journaling. Journaling allows you to keep a detailed record of your emotions at any given time. It is beneficial to go back and see what progress you have made or what you need to go back and revisit that you may have missed. Meditation is a fantastic tool since it helps to relax your mind and allows you to see clearly what needs to be handled. Everything becomes jumbled up at times, and it's difficult to separate life from what we need to confront and work on individually. You will grow enthusiastic as you make time because it will feel good to comprehend the hurt and pain that has been suppressed for so long.

When you find what works for you and know how to use it, and when you know what doesn't, it's not like a cloud opens and you're perfect, but what does happen is that you feel so much better, you're happier, and as time goes on, you address other areas that require your time and energy, and before you know it, you've discovered gifts and knowledge that you didn't even know were a part of you. It may seem overwhelming at first, but as you embrace your personalized path, you will realize that life is a classroom and that everywhere you go, you may either learn something or contribute to the experience. Life is genuinely a journey meant to be savored and shared, not rushed and anxious over how you're going to get to the next moment. Everything we need is right in front of us if we just slow down and pay attention, and God ensures that you can handle any hurdle that may come your way. Pay attention to everything that happens and, most importantly, have fun and breathe throughout the process of receiving the present.

It's incredible what we protect ourselves from, and even more incredible that we do a lot of it unknowingly. After a while of doing things, we are merely on auto-pilot and no second thought is given to the why, when, what, or where of it all. You've just been surviving as best you could under the conditions that have essentially gotten you to where you are today. Is this really where you want to be? Or have you always thought there had to be more? You are exactly on track if you are where you want to be, but if you aren't, you have already begun to take the steps by getting this far. If you've always thought that there must be more, you're still on the correct track. There's nothing wrong with striving for more. Unfortunately, many of us were socialized to believe that there isn't enough for everyone and that asking for more is selfish and/or greedy. This is not true from a variety of perspectives, one of which is how do you explain the reality that there are people who have so much in their lives that they waste it, and it doesn't have to be money, food, or space. It could be anything that is plentiful. Every day, we hear tales of people suffering or goods being thrown away that could have been used or reused, and then there are the stories in the center that create a balance between the two. The goal remains to let go and break free from your prior way of thinking.

# Chapter 4: New Focus

What now that you realized that nothing is set in stone and that you do have a say in what your life will become and what you want out of life? Now is the moment to examine every aspect of your personality. What constitutes the absolute essence of who you are? When you do this, you are not only learning to love yourself on a level you have never experienced before, but you are also opening the door to a more open, loving, tranquil existence that is very different from what you have lived up to this point. Doing the work to understand about yourself will reveal things you never considered before, such as why your favorite color is blue, grey, or green. How did you get that nickname? And what is it that makes you so sensitive to particular topics and conversations? All of these things are powerful and will make you feel whole and complete as you embark on this road of not only self-discovery but also whole life renovation. The question "am I chasing someone else's dream?" will not only make sense, but you will also begin to understand what your genuine desire, passion, or purpose is. Knowing this is revolutionary because you will finally be on the way to discovering who you truly are and what you truly want to do. You lost sight of yourself somehow along the way, and now you are recovering not only your life, but also the freedom to be truly you, which is a beautiful celebration in and of itself.

During this time, life will still happen and you will still contrast the difference is that you will know that the terrible days are preparing you for better days ahead and you will not get so caught up in trying to solve every problem. Having more tranquility in your life is a beautiful thing, and being open to learning can allow you to learn and participate in new experiences every day. Additionally, practicing gratitude is critical to your overall growth as an individual and as a family unit. How can you grumble when you're surrounded by such beautiful splendor? If you're stuck in an office, set your screensaver to a stunning sunset or a favorite photo. If you want to go away from the digital world, imagine a lovely image that brings a smile to your face every time you think about it. And, whenever your day seems a bit too hectic, focus on something that takes you away from that moment, even if just for a few seconds. This will interrupt the cycle of negativity and allow you to find calm, from which you may move on. Do not allow yourself to be dragged into a state of despair. Break the chain minute by minute, or even second by second if necessary. Meditation can also help to quiet and soothe the mind in this situation.

From school to work, we have been programmed to work ourselves like machines. For many years of our lives, we are compelled to repeat the same acts. Many times, our lives are dictated by alarm clocks and timers that tell us when to return to the daily grind. Change your life's narrative and make everything as joyful as possible within reason. Enjoy the little things and don't get too worked up about things you can't change. And when it comes time to have fun, fill the time with everything you can and be fully present in the moment, not on social media or in the argument that was going on before you left, but in the moment that you are experiencing right then and there, and as it comes to a close, take mental pictures and maybe even journal to go back and experience it again as often as you want. It has become normal practice to magnify the negative and make the positive seem little and remote. We've got it backwards. Ride them like waves through the ripples of your life, just as you did in the good times. Every day will be an experience, and you will be drawn to where you put your attention. You have the unique potential to direct your own destiny. Be open to new things and fresh beginnings, and lock the door on everything that does not help you get closer to your destiny.

Setting these boundaries in your life will only serve to reinforce the greater significance that you have placed on your life. Many will be perplexed at first, and the majority will have something to say. It will almost certainly be a mixed mixture of favorable and negative feedback. Just like the masterpiece you created as a child that you knew would be revolutionary in your family, but it didn't get half the attention it needed. This situation will reoccur, but this time you will be able to see your entire potential, which makes it so tough to continue. The only difference now is that you've found peace and realized that there's not just more to you than you thought, but also to life than you ever imagined. It's an age-old legend. Someone has an idea, but no one else sees it. They just cannot grasp the concept that is being offered to them. It's just too strange for them, and they think they're protecting you by encouraging you to decrease your expectations. However, as you begin to see success, everyone wants to be a part of it. They knew you'd make it but didn't want to put you under too much pressure. We both know that they truly believed you would fail and were just waiting for the crash. Not everyone will see or feel what you are feeling, which is fine because the only person who needs to be totally present is you.

# Chapter 5: Capture a dream

This is the phase when you may have fun because you may not have realized you were chasing someone else's dream when you started. With all due respect, it may have been their dream for you with the best of intentions, but we should all select our own aspirations. Actually, our dreams select us, and we simply fill in all of the potential needed to meet the obligations required to make the dream a reality. Life will always lead you in the right direction. The difficulty is to listen, pay attention, and stay on track because, as we all know, life can be a rollercoaster ride that goes quicker and faster at times and slower as a snail crossing the pavement on a dewy autumn morning at others. This is also how our dreams unfold. It will now always be victory after victory. There will be disappointments and defeats. You're just wise enough to realize that those things were meant to point you in the right direction and provide additional inspiration. And when things are going well, appreciate them for what they are. Remember the sentiments, the color of the dress or suit you wore, the passion you had to create everything that went into the staging of those events. Give yourself credit for your victories, accept criticism from your defeats, and move on.

Not every situation necessitates intense concentration. Some experiences are supposed to pass as swiftly as they arrived. It is also critical to learn to tell the difference. Maintain your humility and kindness, and when you encounter like-minded people, hang on to them because they are a source of motivation like no other. You'll attract more and more individuals who feel the same way you do, and each of you will bring something to the table that could be the missing piece of a jigsaw that needs to be solved. These are significant moments because they not only reinforce that you are on the right track and heading in the right direction, but they also make you realize that you are not the only one dealing with these challenges. It's strange to think that there are billions of individuals on the planet and that most of the time we have nothing in common with the majority of them. Things frequently start off pretty well and promising, but then one red flag after another appears, and you have no choice but to walk away. This is very different. This is similar to meeting someone who seems to understand where you're coming from. They not only comprehend, but when you speak with them, they affirm that they understand simply by the way they reply and how smoothly the talks seem to take on a life of their own, and before you know it, hours have passed and it seems like you just struck up a conversation.

This is your community. They don't have to be right next to one other. Sometimes you have the most amazing connections and relationships with people you don't even know, and they are such terrific cheerleaders in your triumphs, and they can be a great resource to call on when things are going so well. With all of your new ideas and thoughts, it can be daunting, but if you focus on one thing at a time, you can accomplish so much. And before you know it, what had been a distant concept for years has become your new favorite activity or past time, bringing you immense delight and connecting you to a community of others who appreciate your talent as well. As I previously stated, perhaps singing has always been a passion of yours, but you lacked the confidence to let anybody hear you outside of the shower or the little mini-concerts you enjoy in the vehicle on the way to work, school, etc. What could it hurt to give something you actually appreciate a little space in your life? If playing games was your favorite pastime and you are still really excellent at it, why not put that talent to use and test how good you truly are? If you really want to give it a moment of your attention, there is a space and a place for everything of interest. Finally, if you adore the outdoors, if everything about it beckons you, why have you not pursued it more deeply? There is so much more to life than riding the predictable hamster wheel and praying for a change. You must be the change you want to see, and one step at a time, you may achieve your goals.

It is not work when we operate from a place of love and passion. It's like waking up in your favorite episode of your favorite program, or hearing your favorite song at just the right volume at just the right time. It just feels nice, and everyone could benefit from it. Breaking the pattern of what others want, expect, and desire from you is true freedom, and no one on this planet can give or take it away from you, but you have the incredible capacity to create it for yourself anytime you're ready. The emotion of it all will tell you that things are going to be terrific. You can simply think about it and create a whole scenario to support that concept. Please keep in mind that no idea is good or bad. You simply have to pick through all of the ideas that are flying through your mind until you locate the ones that are as bright as sunshine. These are the concepts or thoughts that bring you delight or make you smile just thinking about them. Have you ever come to a fork in the road, or simply a crossroads, when everything seemed impossible? You just weren't sure which direction to go, so you either were overwhelmed by everything in front of you, or you took a few steps back to balance the pros and drawbacks before making a decision. Perhaps you meditated on the concept of gaining a clear vision, and then the path you needed to take became so plain that you couldn't believe it was so simple and right in front of you the entire time. Even back then, you'd exaggerated and made things far more difficult than they needed to be. We complicate the basic and downplay the complicated as humans.

# Chapter 6: Embracing Clarity

Somehow, we got it into our brains that dreams were linked to fame and wealth, and if that's your wish, it can be, but you can also agree on a dream that you have formed long ago by simply giving it power and only the moments of your time that you can spare over time, and you will have a bright vibrate piece of yourself that's all yours. Dreams are whatever we make them, and unfortunately, most of us think of these fantastic, daring things in our youth, and they stay there. Because that is where the disconnect occurred, and you lost sight of what it was that you truly desired for yourself, and at some point you decided that it was too late to try or go for that dream or dreams because it no longer fits you, or you just have so much going on in your life that a dream seems too much like a fairy tale, so you just stay in the realm of the life you have created around the programming, traumas, and goals that you have added along the way. This is known as surviving, and you have been in survival mode since the tear in your fabric happened, and you didn't even notice it until that tear became a visible rip, allowing you to not only see but also feel the empty space where something should be. We frequently feel as if something is simply missing. We can't quite put our finger on it, but something isn't quite right, and we've tried numerous things for years, believing they'd suit the bill, but they never seem to be precisely what we need. I'm sure you know other people who get the same feeling that something isn't quite right.

To cope, we sometimes try to dull the experience, which sends you on an entirely new path. For many, autopilot is always on standby.

For others, you're continually trying the newest item, expecting that it'll be the one, just to discover that it doesn't work. It's now becoming OK to admit that things need to change and that we typically require assistance. We frequently seek the answer alone because no one knows what we are looking for or they have so much judgement in place that explaining would feel like a drawn-out court battle. Clarity is a blessing because it allows you to see things for what they are, but it also has a way of showing us things we have been avoiding or simply don't want to know. In any case, paving the way for new energy will be difficult, but it will be worthwhile. And when you accomplish your objectives one by one, you'll be glad you never gave up on yourself and put the time, energy, and effort in yourself. Remember to recharge, when necessary, by adopting methods to quiet and center yourself so that you are not overwhelmed. Continue even if no one else sees what you see. Not everyone will understand, and there's a reason for that. You would not have gone through the adventures and lessons you did to get to where you are if everyone could see and comprehend your dreams. This is a personal path that each of us must take in our own way and at our own pace throughout our lives.

Remember to keep your life in balance. You will still have your daily ups and downs, as well as your victories and lessons that come with it all. Don't compare your situation to anyone else's. This is the quickest way to reverse the progress you have made. The good news is that you do not drop out. You simply use it as a guidepost on your journey. We never know what others are going through, so why not be as optimistic as possible in all facets of our lives? Not only are joy and happiness addicting, but it also feels nice to witness others living happily as they face their own set of challenges and journeys. Life has a way of producing more of what we put into it, so remember that if you're usually angry, unpleasant, and irritated, you're not only producing it, but you're also receiving it. And it is extremely easy to get caught up in a cycle of negativity and not know how to break free. Fortunately, we've spoken about how to interrupt negative cycles and create a happy generator that we can use anytime we need it. You will begin to obtain more the instant you decide that you want, desire, and deserve more. It's like sending an SOS out into the cosmos and saying "help me," and the universe answers by saying "send me a vibration of what you want," and you'll see major and subtle changes all throughout your life. Each one is unique, yet profound.

www.ingramcontent.com/pod-product-compliance
Lightning Source LLC
LaVergne TN
LVHW020544160826
845677LV00015B/4203

* 9 7 9 8 8 4 8 5 5 4 9 8 4 *